HIT THE SPOT
How to Tame the Currency Market

Reggie Henkart
Forex Trainer

No part of this publication may be reproduced, stored in a retrieval system, or transmitted in any form or by any means, electronic, mechanical, photocopying, recording, scanning, or otherwise, except as permitted under Section 107 or 108 of the 1976 United States Copyright Act, without either the prior written permission of the Publisher, or authorization through payment of the appropriate per-copy fee to the Copyright Clearance Center, Inc. Requests to the Publisher for permission should be addressed to Family Freedom, Inc., Fax: (415) 382-7757.

ISBN-13: 978-0-9720738-4-4
ISBN-10: 0-9720738-4-1

Printed in the United States of America

Acknowledgment

I could not have written this book without the unconditional support, trust and love of my wife, Andrea. Not only is she a brilliant speaker, but she is truly a master in the MLM industry, with almost ten thousand people in her downline. Additionally, she has always given me the space I needed, whether it was to write this book, sail in the Caribbean, or play golf with my buddies. I feel very fortunate to be married to her for over 26 years.

Disclaimer

- Leveraged foreign exchange trading carries a significant level of risk and may not be suitable for all investors. The high degree of leverage may work against you, as well as for you. Before deciding to invest in foreign exchange, carefully consider your investment objectives, level of experience and risk appetite. Be aware of all the risks associated with foreign exchange trading and seek advice from an independent financial advisor if you have any doubts.

- The contents provided in this book are subject to change at any time without notice, and are provided for the sole purpose of assisting traders to make independent investment decisions. We have taken reasonable measures to ensure the accuracy of the information, however, we cannot guarantee its accuracy, and will not accept liability for any loss or damage, which may arise directly or indirectly from the content or as a result of strategies given. There is no guarantee that the systems, trading techniques, trading methods, indicators or other information presented in this book will result in profits or losses. You, the user of the techniques, are responsible for your own actions, and need to decide whether or not to use the materials and ideas. The content is provided for informational purposes only and is not intended as a trading recommendation.

- CFTC RULE 4.41 states that "Hypothetical or simulated performance results have certain limitations unlike an actual performance record. Simulated results do not represent actual trading. Also, since the trades have not been executed, the results may have under-or-over compensated for the impact, if any, or certain market factors, such as lack of liquidity. Simulated trading programs in general are also subject to the fact that they are designed with the benefit of hindsight. No representation is being made, that any account will, or is likely to, achieve profit or losses similar to those shown."

- The techniques, ideas and materials in this book are copywritten and proprietary. Reggie Henkart is an Independent Representative of FreedomRocks, Inc. The contents of this book have not been approved or reviewed by FreedomRocks, Inc. and do not in any way represent their views, opinions or policies.

Table of Contents

Introduction

Abbreviation of the currencies used:

EUR = Euro used in Europe

GBP = Great British Pound used in the British Isles

CHF = Confédération Helvetica Franc used in Switzerland

JPY = Japanese Yen used in Japan

USD = United States Dollar

Broker's Platform:

In this book, the platform being used is from InterbankFX (IBFX), the Forex broker. All indications are based on the MetaTrader 4 (MT4). Throughout the book, you will see brackets: [ ], which refer to the MT4 instructions.

To get the proper version and leverage I use, [go to *www.fxez.biz*. Select "Open Live Account" and fill your information to get your account ID number (no money needed at this time) but you'll be ready when you want to transfer the funds. Then click on "Open Demo," select MT4 and a Standard Account. Download the platform then, finally, choose "400:1" leverage and the amount you want to practice with.]

For more information on IBFX, call 866-468-3739.

The smart man learns from his mistakes,
The wise man learns from the mistakes of others.

Chinese Proverb

Part 1
READY

I. What's in it for You?

In any market, there are Traders and Investors.

The Trader is like a hunter, waiting patiently for the kill. He wants the thrill of studying the Technicals, looking at his myriad of exciting indicators. He keeps checking his system, studying the currency prices, as they appear, hour after hour, minute after minute, in a beautiful dance around the various colors of different indicators. He looks at patterns and crossing lines of moving averages. He *feels* the market and smiles, as he gets ready to take a bite out of the immensity of this two trillion dollar a day market. He is making sure his stop loss is where he wants it; not too close to get hit by the market noise, but close enough to protect his equity if the market goes against his judgment. He knows this may happen often, perhaps as often as he wins. That is why his losses are short and he continues to ride the wave of his winnings as long as he can.

The Investor also knows that his speculation may not always win. He feels that he has to be right only four times out of ten. However, the four times will pay substantially more than what he would have lost. He doesn't stare at the computer. He has no need to. He makes his calculations once or twice a week, maybe slightly more in volatile markets.

His phone will vibrate with a text message letting him know one of his pending orders has been hit. No sweat, he has time. Even if he does nothing, his account will still make money. The interest will accumulate steadily every day, giving him a return of 20-85% at the end of the year, while his equity is virtually hedged at 97-98%.

Before going to sleep, he will adjust his positions and prepare for the next market move.

> *It was never my thinking that made the big money for me. It was my sitting.*
>
> Jesse Livermore
> Notable Stock Trader

II. Why the Spot Currency Market?

There are so many markets to invest in. They include stocks, futures, options and real estate. I prefer the Spot Currency market (also called Foreign Exchange market, Cash Currency market, or Forex) over all of the others. This market is so attractive and has carried an explosion of success in the last decade, since the accessibility of the web. Let's compare with the stock market as it seems to be the closest competitor.

- Forex is the biggest market in the world: approximately two trillion dollars traded daily
- Only six major currencies instead of thousands of stocks
- Liquidity guaranteed
- Interest paid every day
- Forex market cannot be manipulated
- Transparent market; no "accounting discrepancies"
- Gaps are very seldom
- Little or no slippage on orders
- Huge volume creates best Technical analysis
- Parity market makes them swing rather than crash or split

- No brokerage fees, you only pay the spread between the Bid and the Ask
- Very little possibility of owing more than the Equity at risk

Personally, I do not like Forex options. Imagine trading currency options on a 9 to 5 basis (EST) when the underlying currency is trading 24 hours a day. Imagine being at the mercy of worldwide events after the market closes every day.

If this peaks your interest, please read more on this in *Characteristics and Risks of Standardized Options* by the American Stock Exchange, LLC, Chicago Board Options Exchange, Incorporated, New York Stock Exchange, Inc., NYSE Arca, Inc. and Philadelphia Stock Exchange, Inc. (1994).

"The Interbank market in foreign currencies is a global, around-the-clock market. Therefore, the hours of trading for foreign currency options do not conform to the hours during which the underlying currencies are traded. To the extent that the options markets are closed while the market for the underlying currencies remains open, significant price and rate movements may take place in the underlying markets that cannot be reflected in the options markets. The possibility of such movements should be taken into account in relating closing prices in the options markets to those in the underlying markets.

In addition, this creates a risk that foreign currency options may be exercised on the basis of price movements in the underlying currency after the close of trading in the options markets, when writers are no longer able to close out their short positions."

III. Technicals vs. Fundamentals

There are two different worlds in the foreign currency market analysis: Fundamental and Technical.

The Fundamentalist reads every single paper and financial magazine. He listens to every piece of news to find out what is happening in the world and how it can influence currencies. Interest rates will have no secrets for the Fundamentalist, neither will the Gross Domestic Product (GDP). Phone in hand, he awaits the Non-Farm Payroll with vibrant expectation.

Only a brave man or a fool predicts exchange rates.
                                        The Economist, April 2006

The Technician, or Chartist, is ready as well, but for different reasons. He uses Technicals. He studies his maps. He measures every single indicator he loves working with. He is prepared. He places his entry order, his stop is ready and he knows where he will make his profit. To him, looking at his chart is like looking at a piece of art. Colors, lines and curves dance around Candlesticks that represent mass human behavior.

I encourage you to use both methods, as it will result in a bigger picture. However, the information you can gather in your charts far surpasses, in my opinion, what you can gather in the news. Charts reveal the past, the present and, somewhat, the future.

When a person with experience meets a person with money, pretty soon, the person with experience will have the money and the person with money will have the experience.

Estee Lauder

IV. Basic Technicals

My goal here is to show you which indicators I use and why. The purpose of this section is not to teach every single trading indicator, as there are many books available which do that very well. I have included some of these books in my preferred reading list at the end of this manual.

1. Basic Pattern Analysis

You can see the five most important basic pattern analysis in Fig. 1 & 2:
- Trend Lines (Fig.1)
- Channels (Fig. 1)
- Support and Resistance (Fig. 1)
- Triangles and Pennants (Fig.1)
- Double/Triple Bottom/Tops (Fig. 2)

Fig. 1

Fig. 2

Each analysis gives you a visual image where prices form a pattern. It is a direct reflection of the market's psychology. The idea is to invest as if the pattern will continue, using the direction as a target and protecting yourself with a stop loss if it does not follow through.

If you look at the Channel on Fig. 1, a Support is when prices consolidate on the bottom (floor). Resistance is when it occurs at the top (ceiling). Many times, when prices cross these lines, Support may become Resistance and vice versa.

2. Candlesticks

I was exposed to Candlesticks in 1993, thanks to my Chinese teachers. That was on DOS when the feed was approximately $4,000 a month. At that time, almost every Trader was using the normal bar charts, but I could see the visuals that only the Candlesticks could offer.

Fig. 3

There are many types of Candlesticks. Some of them reveal a picture on their own, others show it in a group. An example of my favorite, the Doji, shows a retracement. It has a short body and sometimes has long wicks. Imagine an extended + sign. Check out how the trend turned around in Fig. 3 after almost every Doji. If the trend goes down, the Doji may change the direction of the market and it could go back up.

There are no indicators that will always be 100% correct and the longer the time frame, the more solid the signal.

In other words, a weekly signal will have more meaning than a 30-minute signal.

There are many more signs you can learn about. A great place to start is with the book, *"The Candlestick Course,"* by Steve Nison (Wiley 2003). You can also go to <u>*www.candlecharts.com*</u> to find his complete line of educational products.

> *Candlesticks analysis is not rocket science. It is simple investment philosophy put into a visual graphic.*
> Stephen Bigalow
> Author of *Profitable Candlestick Trading*

3. Indicators

There are a myriad of indicators available. Some are free, some are costly and some are outrageously expensive. My favorite indicator is free but takes time to trust because it is built on experience. It is called **Intuition.** After a while, you will be able to just look at a chart and *"know"* where it will go. I encourage you to include Intuition in your palette of preferred indicators.

I invite you to try this exercise: Open a Demo account (that is an account that uses virtual money) and just use your Intuition. You may be surprised at how good you become.

Markets either Trend (go up and down) or Channel (go sideways). Here are the indicators I use in either case.

a. Trending Markets

I use four **Moving Averages (M.A.):** Simple 8, 13, 34 and 200.

[Go to Insert>Indicators>Trend>Moving Average and select the above numbers]

The idea behind this is to see when the price crosses the M.A. or when they cross each other. A Moving Average may also serve as a Support or a Resistance.

There is an interesting situation that occurs when each Moving Average crosses the next one in the same direction. If the 8 crosses above the 13, which crosses above the 34 M.A., which then crosses above the 200 M.A., you are in for a strong uptrend (Fig. 4). The opposite would be true if each one crosses below the next. That would suggest a nice downtrend.

For more information on all indicators, I recommend reading, *"Technical Analysis of the Financial Markets"* by John Murphy (NYIF 1999).

Fig. 4

I also use **Parabolics** in trending markets because it typically shows a retracement.

[Go to Insert>Indicators>Trend>Parabolic SAR]

Parabolics tell the Trader to reverse his position. If he was buying, he should sell, and vice versa. I don't use it this way, because it is not as effective in non-trending markets. However, I do recognize it could help you forecast an ending trend.

18

The Partabolic dots are chaging directions coupled with other indicators may show a retracement

Fig. 5

More recently, I added **ADX** to my myriad of indicators.

[Go to Insert>Indicators>Trend>Average Directional Movement Index]

According to Charles Schaap, in his ADX Reversal Patterns article in the March 2007 issue of *Technical Analysis of Stocks & Commodities* magazine (a must read for all Traders), he measures the trend strength by looking at the ADX line. A value of 25 and above is a strong indication that the trend will continue.

Below 25 means it is getting weaker and may suggest a retracement or worse, a reversal. If the +DMI is over the –DMI, the trend is up, otherwise it's down. These are the ADX basics I look at.

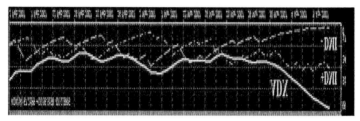

Fig. 6

b. Non-trending markets (Channeling)

I use a Fibonacci (see next section) version of **MACD**: 13, 21, 8. This Technical offers different strategies. Not only does it include a Moving Average crossover (which is actually an average of an M.A.), but a histogram that reveals convergences and divergences in that market. It is interesting to compare trend lines you would trace between MACD histogram hills and trend lines you create with the actual currency prices. It has a touch of forecasting ability. The difference with the default setting is not huge. I fine-tuned it and it works a little faster.

[Go to Insert>Indicators>Oscillators>MACD, then replace 12, 26 and 9 by 13, 21 and 8]

In a Channeling market, I also use **Stochastics,** which provide me with an overbought/oversold situation.

[Go to Insert>Indicators>Oscillators>Stochastic Oscillators]

In Fig. 7, towards the second week of March 2007, the Stochastics were in a strong overbought position (above 80). After that, the market went down substantially.

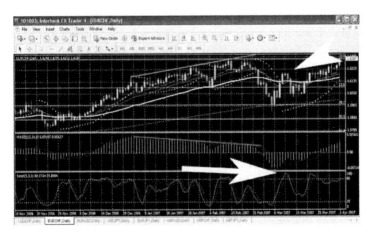

Fig. 7

> *Stochastics measures the momentum of price. If you visualize a rocket going up in the air – before it can turn down, it must slow down. Momentum always changes direction before price.*
>
> George Lane
> Technical Analyst

4. Fibonacci

In the late 12th century, mathematician Leonardo de Pisa (a.k.a. Fibonacci) was playing with numbers and discovered unique ratios and proportions.

Remember the movie, *The DaVinci Code?* The password that opened the safe was 01123581321. You might be wondering how I remembered the password. I started with 0 and 1; 1+0=1 (third number); 1+1=2 (fourth); 2+1=3 (fifth); 3+2=5. Are you getting this? Keep adding the number to the previous one.

Fibonacci (nicknamed Fib or Fibo) divided each number by the number before, and the one after, and so on. The most important ratios he found were 61.8%, 50% and 38.2%.

From these observations, Fibonacci popularized the Golden Ratio, which can be found over and over in our Universe and beyond. A very famous image that illustrates this is the Vitruvian Man which shows the numerical proportions of a human being (Fig. 8).

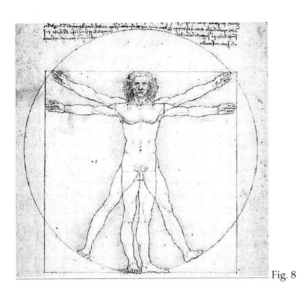

Fig. 8

Major financial mathematicians, such as W.D. Gann and Elliott Wave, decided to adapt these numbers into the financial markets. Today, it is so much easier to trace a Fibonacci retracement with Windows than it was with DOS in the early 1990's.

[Select the chart you are working on. Go to Insert> Fibonacci> Retracement. Put the cursor on the farthest lowest or highest peak and drag the cursor to the most recent lowest or highest peak]

Et voilà! You now have a set of horizontal lines that miraculously seem to match Supports and Resistances as if they were magnets (see Fig. 9).

Fig.9

This is how I use it to predict an uncertain future by "guessing" Supports and Resistances where the price may consolidate.

Once you have set up your Fibo from the top to the bottom, or vice versa for an uptrend, the rest becomes the future. In Fig. 9, it was done on July 2000 (bottom). During the four following years, notice how many times the price became congested on the Fibo lines. They literally bounced on those Resistances and Supports.

This is an interesting phenomenon. Look at how many times a Resistance became a Support once it was forced through. It works the other way around as well.

24

Traders use this indicator very successfully as a forecasting tool to go in or out of trades. These trades are done as a group, which adds to the forecasting effect.

Fig.10

On February 21, 2007, I let go of the Euro.
Fig. 10 shows an example of why I did this:
- Hit a high Fibonacci once
- Hit it for the second time (double top)
- Strong divergence (see uptrend line on chart compared to MACD)

When more people sell or buy at the same time, the psychology kicks in and massive moves are made in the market.

V. VantagePoint

I use VantagePoint (VP) as an indicator that provides me with the direction of where the currency is going the next day. It also projects the high and low of that market at approximately 80% accuracy. This gives me an amazing edge.

Nobody can explain VP better than VP itself. Below, you will find excerpts from the Help File of the software.

(…) means I abridged the text
<…> means I added some comments

"VantagePoint was first released in 1991 by Louis Mendelsohn, a leading trading software pioneer, and revised extensively over the years. It is a very robust trading software program which analyzes individual markets from both a single-market as well as an intermarket perspective. Recognizing the global nature of the world's financial markets and that they can affect each other, VantagePoint looks at the relationships of 25 related markets on each target market, and makes highly accurate trend forecasts based upon the effects of these underlying and often obscure relationships.

 VantagePoint is a user-friendly toolbox of predictive indicators which can augment your current trading approach by adding a broadened intermarket perspective.

Use VantagePoint to stay out of potentially damaging trades, or take potentially profitable trades that you might have previously avoided. (…)

Using the pattern recognition capabilities of neural networks, VantagePoint predicts short, medium, and long-term moving averages for up to four days in the future. Then VantagePoint computes a unique crossover leading indicator based on the difference between the predicted moving average and today's actual moving average. Changes in the value of the crossover leading indicator from one day to the next can help you determine if VantagePoint expects the market to be choppy, maintain its trend, or change trend direction.

VantagePoint anticipates market direction. Often the crossover leading indicator gives an early indication that the market will change direction. Additional independent indicators within VantagePoint may be used to confirm the expected change in trend direction. When all indicators agree, there is a high probability that the market will move in the indicated direction. VantagePoint even predicts the high and low prices for the next day, to help you determine where to set stops, when to tighten up on them and when to close out trades.

VantagePoint also predicts the MACD, RSI and Stochastic values one day in advance. These predictions will be very valuable to technical Traders who use them to anticipate changes in market sentiment, trend reversals, and overbought/oversold conditions. In addition, the Predicted Neural Index predicts if a three-day moving average of the midpoint price will rise or fall in the next two days, giving you additional confirmation regarding the anticipated trend direction.

Position Traders can utilize VantagePoint's predicted highs and lows to help set entry points, and then use the predicted high/low range on subsequent days to adjust daily stops. For example, if you are long on the S&P 500 Index <replace by EUR/CHF> and the market is expected to continue to move up tomorrow, you might set your stop for tomorrow below tomorrow's predicted low. This strategy can help decrease the likelihood of being stopped out prematurely during the day.

The predictions of the next day's high and low can be used to help determine entry and exit points for day trading. If the indicators on the Daily Report suggest that tomorrow is likely to be an up day, day Traders can wait for the market to trade down toward the projected low, then enter a long position which might then be closed out intraday at or near the projected high. The reverse would involve entering a short position at or near the projected high on a day expected to be down. (…)

VantagePoint opens the door of intermarket analysis to both novice and experienced Traders. It provides a powerful set of predictive analysis tools which can be of tremendous benefit to day and position Traders in both the stock and futures markets <and Forex> looking for a competitive edge."

To learn more about this program, go to: *www.tradertech.com* or call 800-732-5407. A sales representative will show you some free samples of recent forecasts.

In addition, www.TradingEducation.com is a good (free) resource for Forex Traders. I also recommend www.TraderChat.com, a free online community for Forex Traders.

Fig. 11 and 12 are charts provided by VantagePoint Trading Software (*www.TraderTech.com*)

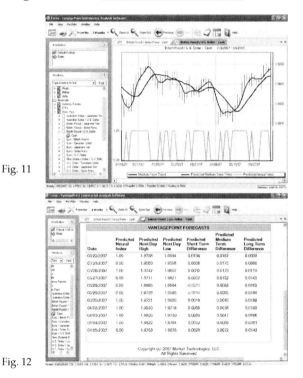

Fig. 11

Fig. 12

VI. Systems

> *Unless the plan says, 'I'll stay until I'm scared'… Stay!*
> Ed Ponsi
> Forex Educator

I have an infinite respect for Professional Forex Day Traders. One of my associates never cared where his Equity was and had no idea, at any given moment, if he was making or losing money. He just followed a system. He may have counted the pips (smallest amount of a currency) at the end of the shift, but he trusted the system he had backtested and went for it.

If you want to be detached and trade as a Trader or an Investor, instead of a gambler, you must have a trading system in place. This system should be one you trust that has proven itself over time in the market. You can rely on it even when your Equity goes down, and continues to go down. We call that a *drawdown*. Every system has a certain amount of drawdown. Expect it as a *when* not an *if*.

Now, that doesn't mean you won't lose any money; it only means when you lose, you lose a little and when you win, you win big. Alternately, it may mean your losses and gains will be equal, but you will win more often. It is better if you have a system that does both.

> *It doesn't matter how often you are right or wrong – it only matters how much you make when you are right, versus how much you lose when you are wrong.*
>
> George Soros
> Global Financier

It's important to figure out what kind of Trader you want to be. This has to do with the time frame you choose. I am, what the industry calls, a Position Trader. I look at Weekly and Daily charts. If you start looking at, or below, the Hourly charts, you are most likely a Day Trader.

> *There are a very small percentage of currency Traders today who make money intraday... You are not going to change that statistic.*
>
> Dirk DuToit
> Author of *Bird Watching in Lion Country*

There are many systems around. The most famous of the numerous systems used today, **Channeling**, takes advantage of the price staying between a Resistance and a Support line. If you look back at Fig. 1, you will notice a situation that looks like Fig. 13.

Fig. 13

The idea is simply to buy at the bottom of the Channel and sell at the top. You may also reverse the situation: sell from the top and buy at the bottom. Place your stop losses slightly below your Support when buying and above the Resistance when selling.

Another system uses an **Engulfing** Candlestick (or Outside Bar) pattern. An Outside Bar has a higher price and a lower price than the previous bar as shown in Fig. 14.

Notice how the trend goes up when the Outside Bar closes higher than it opened and goes down in the opposite case. What I do is buy the currency on the former example when it breaks the high of the Outside Bar, with a 5 Pip Stop Loss below the low of that bar, and vice versa.

Fig. 14

As I mentioned earlier, Systems abound and you have to Demo them first to see how they work. Check the ratio of returns versus losses, the drawdowns (how much you may lose in a row) and the time involved in managing it.

I tried many systems, yet none have come close to what I'm about to reveal next.

Helpful tip:
Keep a journal. Write down why you buy/sell, stop and exit. Keep track of everything, as it may be very useful later when you compare your written comments. See next page for an example of my journal entry.

DATE	4/11/2007
CURRENCY	**B GBP/CHF**
CURRENT PRICE	2.4096
VP INDEX	1
VP HIGH	2.4208
VP LOW	2.4022
ADX	34 +
STOCHASTICS	Up
MACD	Up
MOVING AVERAGES	50 Support
PARABOLIC SAR	Up
FIBO	no
INTUITION	Strong Positive
ENTRY	**2.4057**
STOP LOSS	**2.4010**
PIPS DIFFERENCE	-30
TARGET	**2.4200**
PIPS DIFFERENCE	160
DATE & TIME (GMT)	4/12/07 1403
LOTS	1.00
PRICE ENTRY	2.4057
EXIT DATE & TIME	4/12/07 2313
EXIT PRICE	2.4079
PROFIT/LOSS PIPS	**22**
CARRY TRADE	$16.65
PROFIT/LOSS $	$180.88
COMMENTS AT EXIT	Wait for enter price to trigger

Fig. 15

Part 2
Set

VII. FreedomRocks

In February 2006, I received an email that read, *"Hello Reggie, please check out this link and tell me what you think. Andy."* Normally, I would never waste my time on this type of email, but I thought it was from one of my Forex students. So I checked it out and ran into an amazing program called *FreedomRocks.* I then realized I didn't have an "Andy" in my student database. I called him to find out more about this program and asked him how he got my name. His answer was interesting. He said, *"I googled 'Forex' and your name came up."*

Andy introduced me to the Founder of FreedomRocks, Mark Vincellette. Mark is a genius, a visionary and a very kind man. His program is the easy way, for everybody, to hit the Spot Currency market. It is completely out of the box thinking.

Most Forex brokers tell us that 95% of new Traders kill their accounts in less than 60 days. We are very proud to have thousands of members in FreedomRocks who have never traded in their lives, never heard of a Moving Average or Fibonacci, and still have Live accounts months after doubling or tripling their money.

A FreedomRocks Trader only needs 15 minutes a week to trade any portfolio amount, up to several million dollars. In the past, Traders' profits were at the expense of many sleepless nights. Now we can have a life. As a professional Trader, this is the icing on the cake!

> *With FreedomRocks, you will wake up when you are tired of sleeping.*
>
> Mark Vincellette
> President, FreedomRocks, Inc.

This book is not a FreedomRocks instruction manual. Carole Noxon created amazing step-by-step training webinars for the company, that show people how to use the program. She added various worksheets that simplify an already very simple exercise. Members also have a Forex Training segment particular to the broker they decide to use. So why did I write this manual? Certainly not to change the program, but to fine-tune your entries and exits. I also want to answer most of my students' questions as I have studied this market since 1993.

I also wrote *"Hit the Spot"* for my fellow Traders. I noticed that they quickly got bored looking at the broker's platform for weeks, without intervention. What's more, they complained that, "all this system does is make money."

The fine-tuning I'm about to present to you does not, in any way, shape or form, change the basis of the FreedomRocks program.

Fig. 16 Mark Vincellette at the Dallas conference June 2006.

When I discovered FreedomRocks just before their re-launch, early in 2006, I realized immediately that it was the way to go.

I heard a lot about Carry Trade when I was a Fund Manager in the early 90's. Back then, my Chinese instructors told me, *"Get positive interest regardless of where the currency goes!"*

Many articles were written about the Carry Trade debacle on February 21, 2007.

Kathy Lien, in her comprehensive book, *Day Trading the Currency Market* (Wiley 2006), says, *"…the popularity of Carry Trades has increased significantly over recent years, as Investors are actively seeking high-yielding assets. A Carry Trade involves buying or lending a currency with a high interest rate and selling or borrowing a currency with a low interest rate. With CHF having one of*

41

the lowest interest rates of all industrialized countries, it is one of the primary currencies sold or borrowed in Carry Trades."

Carry Trade means you carry the trade to the next day. By doing that, banks pay you (or charge you) interest on your leveraged amount.

The 'next day' in a 24-hour market will depend on your broker. IBFX decided that 20:59 GMT (4:59pm EST) is when the day changes, when your Candlestick chart creates a new Daily Candlestick and when interest applies.

Meanwhile, if the market goes south and never returns, you may lose a fortune much larger than the interest you collected, even if you received Wednesday's triple interest (this interest is paid three times on that day to cover for the weekend). Therefore, when Mark explained the mirror (or hedge) part of the system to me, I could not believe no one in the industry had thought of that before him, myself included.

Of course, when I started trading in 1993, I didn't really have the same hedge situation as the Deutschmark (DM) was in existence. On January 1, 1999, one EUR replaced 1.9558 DM and the charts were merged.

Today, Mark Vincellette takes advantage of a relationship between the Euro and the Swiss Franc, in a way that many other professional Traders noticed, but didn't know how to use in their favor. All they did was grumble, *"Don't trade these two together. They cancel each other out. You won't make any money!"* Au contraire mon ami, this is exactly where you make your money, big money on a historically mirrored (or hedged) account.

The brilliance of Mark Vincellette's system is to take a relatively well-known strategy in the Forex market called *"Carry Trade investing"* and adapt it to a historically hedged situation.

In a hedged situation, if you buy the Euro and the Franc, it's similar to betting on both Heads <u>and</u> Tales; you come out even. However, with Carry Trade, you receive and pay interest every single day. By choosing the right currencies, the net will be positive and, on a 400:1 leverage, can be pretty big.

The Euro is not the only one mirroring the Franc, the Pound is doing a pretty good job as well. It's a bit more volatile, but it gives so much more interest that you won't want to leave it behind. If you started in the beginning of April 2007, with the Pound against the Franc, with 400:1 at 12.5% margin, you would receive 66.89% a year providing you did nothing else than own this currency pair.

An example of the outstanding possibilities in FreedomRocks occurred while I was overseeing the account of an international celebrity. I helped him generate 50% return in 28 days for a cash return of $105,000 on a $200,000 account. It's not a return you can expect every single month, but we did see it happen a few times in 2006 and in the beginning of 2007. Hopefully, there is more of this in our future.

There are two components to the FreedomRocks software: the Portfolio Allocator and the Portfolio Manager.

1. Portfolio Allocator

Let's start with the choices you have in the Allocator:
- Equity
- Lot size
- Leverage
- Margin Percentage
- Currencies

Inputting this information will take you five minutes maximum.

Obviously, the Equity is your choice. At any time, you can reduce or augment the money at risk in your account, and make choices depending on the situation of the market.

Remember the old adage, *"Only invest money you can afford to lose."* Don't borrow money or use your mortgage or any amount that would change your lifestyle. Diversify!

The program works best with the flexibility of 1k lot size unless you invest more than $50,000.

400:1 leverage is what FreedomRockers prefer, as it will allow you to buy more lots, hence get more interest on the leveraged amount of the currencies you own.

> *When you combine ignorance with leverage, you get some pretty interesting results.*
>
> Warren Buffett
> Third-richest person in the World
> (Forbes April 2007)

The Margin Percentage will be the number one element that determines the buffer, which will allow you to retard a Margin Call. The available choice is between 1% and 30% of the available Equity.

Finally, the currencies will be selected based on the volatility you choose. Out of the four choices: EUR/USD, GBP/USD, USD/CHF AND USD/JPY, I prefer to use the European currencies exclusively.

In my opinion, trading the Yen (USD/JPY) in the FreedomRocks way is more on the gambling side than the investing side. That currency has nothing in common with the European currencies, other than it's pegged to the dollar. The Yen has a very tempting interest rate that lures FreedomRockers into major losses. Don't crash your account, don't trade the Yen.

That leaves us with one at the bottom (Franc) and two at the top (Euro and Pound). While the Euro is a little more stable but pays less interest, the Pound is more volatile and is quite generous. I found that the best of all worlds is to use all three, conveniently nicknamed, *"The Three Amigos."*

I use these selections according to how I perceive the situation in the market and how it affects my portfolio.

What about Stop Losses?
My students will tell you that putting a stop loss is required by "Reggie's Law" (see www.4xez.biz Trader's Declaration). So, why are we not using stops in FreedomRocks? The hedge is what protects us, to a certain extent (97-98% of the time), provided that we give ourselves enough cushion or low Margin Percentage.

I find it very interesting that in FreedomRocks, we have people who are novices, don't know any Technicals and are making money every day throughout the entire year. On the other hand, most newbies, without FreedomRocks, collapse in 90 days.

FreedomRocks takes care of two out of the three important elements of trading: the system and the psychology. The third, Money Management, will be covered later.

What the FreedomRocks program does not do, is prevent you from getting an occasional Margin Call. FreedomRocks is built to preserve your capital. However, let me remind you that there is no Holy Grail in Forex. The industry is wild enough and colossal enough to explode anywhere, at any time.

The catastrophe of 9/11 is an example of this. If you started your investment before the tragedy, your broker would have needed over three times what you had started with to avoid a Margin Call.

Nevertheless, knowing that a Margin Call is not an *if* but a *when,* should make us diligent in our Money Management strategy.

Winners think in terms of how much they can lose; Losers focus on how much they can win.

Larry Pesavento
Trading Tutor

	Lots	Daily Interest	Annual Interest
GBP/USD	1.47	-0.59	-214.62
USD/CHF	2.13	18.91	6,903.54
Total Interest		18.32	6,688.92
% Return on Investment (Interest Only)			66.89 %

Fig.17

The graph in Fig. 17 shows what the Allocator gives you:

- The currencies you chose with the respective amounts of lots (lots are like shares, it's what you buy or sell in the Spot Currency market) and the interest you receive, or pay, on a daily and yearly basis for each of these currencies.
- The total interest and your ROI.

	Lots	Daily Interest	Annual Interest
EUR/USD	0.96	-5.81	-2,119.92
GBP/USD	0.69	-0.27	-100.11
USD/CHF	2.38	21.17	7,728.74
Total Interest		15.09	5,508.71
% Return on Investment (Interest Only)			55.09 %

Fig. 18

To get the best of both worlds, here is how to play the game: get both currencies, the Euro and the Pound against the Franc. *Et voilà,* you have it made. We are now talking a less volatile hedge that will still give an awesome return per year, and this is not even half of what FreedomRocks has to offer.

This is the kind of return that banks get with *your* money. Isn't it time to take control of the return you can get, instead of what the +/- 2% banks give you? Of course, in all fairness, that kind of return is the reward of a hi-risk/hi-return investment.

Fig. 19 My first live trade with FreedomRocks, on a cruise to Puerto Rico March 2006.

FreedomRocks advertises, *"No charts, No guesswork."* Thankfully, IBFX has MetaTrader 4, which they offer for free to anyone.

MetaTrader is extremely complete. If you are a Trader that wants to fine-tune the system, MT4 is a powerful engine. It will provide a more thorough analysis than you will ever need.

2. Portfolio Manager

We have seen the first way to make money in FreedomRocks, using the interest the banks give you just to own the currencies. This, with the number of lots to buy is shown in the Allocator. The FreedomRocks Manager takes care of the second way of making money. It gives you the bracket on the yellow line, which you place above and below each currency (Fig. 20), so you always *buy low* and *sell high* which is a really good thing.

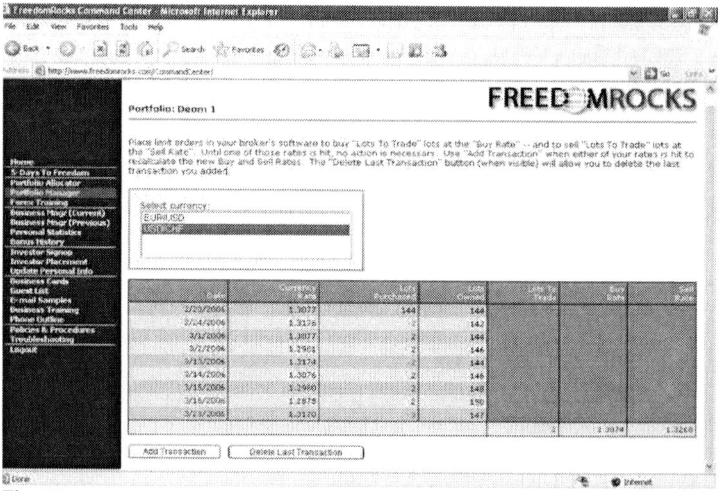

Fig. 20

50

Here is another hint: when you set up the Manager, it will ask you to name your account. You could call it Demo, or My Account, but after a while, you may have quite a few Demos and even a few Live accounts. I name my accounts by the account number given to me in IBFX and my starting Margin Percentage.

Example: 123456 @ 10%

These are the only two elements that the Manager does not store in the program. The rest of the information: date, prices, lots and currencies are there for you to see. You may also want to add the ROI, as it may change with government decisions.

Input the information in your new Porfolio: Equity, Currencies, Lots and actual purchase prices for each Currency. The Portfolio will give you two Pending Orders for each Currency. Place them in MT4 and you are done. This exercise only takes ten minutes.

All you have to do now is to quickly glance at your desktop to check the pending orders before you go to sleep and after you wake up. If they are all there, go about your day. Otherwise, replace the two orders of the currency that have been triggered (a whopping three minutes of work!)

This happens just three or four times per week, on average, for a total of 12 to 15 minutes of work each week, regardless of the size of the investment.

Some Traders like to have a warning on their cell phone or receive an email when the pending order is triggered. You can request these options at www.alertfx.com.

Sell Orders

One of the issues people seem to struggle with in IBFX, is knowing how to handle a sell order. The principal is relatively simple. When a pending sell is triggered, FreedomRocks wants you to deduct it from the batch you own.

An example of this may be that you own 50 lots of GBP/USD. Your 2 lots sell order triggers. You should have 48 lots left. Unless you use the IBFX-Rocks template, the broker will actually open a sell order. Therefore, as far as the broker is concerned, you have 50 buys and 2 sells, not 48. To resolve that, close your sell order (right click and close). Then, close 2 of the 50 lots you own (right click, close, change the volume from 0.50 to 0.02). Finally, select close again. Et voilà, you will have the 48 lots the Portfolio Manager expects you to own.

Just a note: InterbankFX states, *"The IBFX-Rocks consists of a custom indicator and expert advisor that we have created as companions to the FreedomRocks trading system."*

[Go to http://www.interbankfx.com/rocks/]

Feel free to learn more about this tool. As it is computer based, which means your computer has to be on at all times, it doesn't really work for me. I trade from a laptop that travels as much as I do.

Now this gets really exciting. So far, I have shown you the traditional way of trading in the first part of this book. I have covered the amazing tools offered by FreedomRocks in Part 2. In this next section, I want to show you how I have put it all together.

> *A good trading system and the mental strength to commit to and execute the signals that system gives you is the way of the seasoned trader.*
>
> Norman Hallett
> Author of *Mental Fitness For Traders*

Part 3
Go!

VIII. ENTRY & EXIT STRATEGIES

This is a sample of what I do before I decide to go in or out of the market.

1. I like to have a few Fundamentals, so I check www.FxStreet.com (where I occasionally host a webinar on trading) and www.Dailyfx.com.
2. I look at the overall Technical picture (weekly and daily charts), as some patterns or trends may come up. I check the ADX and Parabolic indicators. This provides me with my first set of clues.
3. In VantagePoint, I look at the prediction for the currencies at stake.
4. Fibo gives me my next clue. It shows me where I am, relative to those Supports and Resistances, and how the currencies are moving between them.
5. I look at the Candlesticks carefully as they have so much to tell me in terms of retracements.
6. Lastly, I do look at the Averages, MACD and Stochastics.

I come from a school where all tools were charted on DOS (before Windows). This limitation forced me to look at a bird's eye view of the market.

I believe that this perspective offers so much more information than any particular indicator.

Earlier, I mentioned "Triple Interest Day," which is a favorite of the FreedomRockers. It happens every Wednesday at 4:59PM EST. You must buy the currencies that start with USD: USD/CHF (& USD/YEN if you have to) before that time. Buy the currencies that end with USD: EUR/USD and GBP/USD after that time. Your only risk is that you will not be hedged for a few minutes in a market that is usually extremely slow (it's in Australia at that time). You will get paid three times the positive interest and none of the negative interest. This is quite a deal.

You can also receive Triple Interest when you exit the trade by doing the opposite. On Wednesday, close your EUR and GBP before 4:59PM EST, then CHF and YEN after.

> *Simplicity is the mother of perfection.*
>
> Victor Avila
> Master Photographer

At this point, you may have already figured out one of the following conditions:
1. You are hitting a Resistance: price may go down
2. You are hitting a Support: price may go up

3. Neither of the above has occurred
4. You are amazed about your recent profit (25% in 2-3 weeks)

It's important to have this figured out if you use the right chart. Which chart are you looking at, the Pound, the Euro or the Franc? You should not be looking at either one because in FreedomRocks, those are not what you are really trading. If you are trading the EUR/USD against the USD/CHF, you need to look at the EUR/CHF. Why? Take off the common numerator/denominator of these pairs and you will notice you are actually trading the cross currency EUR/CHF.

In fact, I raised this issue in June 2006, when I spoke at the FreedomRocks conference in Dallas, TX. I showed a comparison of the EUR/CHF chart after switching from Candlesticks to Line mode with the Equity of my account, also in a Line mode in Excel (Fig. 22). I could have traded the EUR/USD against the USD/CHF, as it was almost the same graph. **You could actually trade the Equity!**

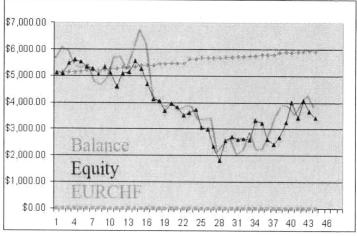

Fig. 22

The same can be said for the GBP/USD against the USD/CHF. You need to look at the cross currency GBP/CHF. However, if you are using both the Euro and the Pound against the Franc, you will need to look for a clue by also analyzing the EUR/CHF, since no charts combine the Three Amigos.

Balance vs. Equity
As one of the top leaders in FreedomRocks, I receive countless emails from Traders asking me about the difference between their Equity and their Balance.

By using FreedomRocks, you will notice that the Balance always goes up. It accumulates the profits from the closed trades, as we always buy low and sell high. The only exceptions I have encountered are on holidays in the country I was trading the currency in.

You may have a temporary lower Balance if your broker includes interest in your Balance, as the country won't pay you interest on holidays. The other exception would be if you *trade* the FreedomRocks system by selecting entries and exits, using the traditional way.

The Equity represents your open positions in the market and will be above or below the Balance or your entry point. That is the amount you will end up with if you close all your positions.

I respect what the FreedomRocks Allocator and Manager assign to me and have one hundred percent trust in it. My friend, Mark Vincellette and I, have similar trading philosophies. Mark will tell you **not** to change anything in the program. He says it is fine as it is. It's an investment that, in the long run -- at least nine months, according to Mark -- should be extremely effective and lucrative.

You don't **need** to do anything else, which is why it is a no-guesswork, no-charts system. However, if you want to have fun adding to the FreedomRocks system, it is up to you, the individual Trader.

A few Traders, however, have gone to the extent of changing the numbers given by the Allocator and the Manager.

In my opinion, there is no need to change a formula that is working well.

To fine-tune this situation without jeopardizing the FreedomRocks program and the levels it provides, let's discuss two main possibilities:
1. Your Equity just made a lot of money.
2. Your Equity just lost a lot of money.

1. Your Equity Just Made a Lot of Money

a. Close your account, get a paycheck and re-allocate.

Here is an example of what I mean. You start with $35,000. A month later, you are over $49,000. You can take $14,000 away and re-allocate with the initial $35,000. Understand that, upon re-entry, you will pay the spreads (fees to the broker).

Unless you *physically* get some money out of the account, it will still be at risk on a Margin Call. Most brokers don't have a "parking place" where you can hold your money out of the market. You can open a new account with the broker, transfer the money and not trade it; or just have them wire the funds to your bank or send you a check.

b. Adjust your Margin Percentage.
Example: The GBP/CHF is trading between 2.3500 and 2.3750. It just hit 2.3783. Your Margin

Percentage was at 12.5% and you want to reduce it to 7.5%.

Because of this surge, you notice you are hitting a Resistance, but the channel is pretty narrow, so you just want to reduce your Margin Percentage. Normally, you would close all positions and re-allocate. However, you want to re-enter a relatively similar amount, so you just add or subtract the difference between the two allocations. It will be much cheaper in your brokerage fees.

Check the Allocator as if you are entering the new parameters with the reduced Margin Percentage. That should give you the required lots to buy. All you need to do is sell off the excess lots. It is important to know that this may lower your Balance momentarily.

Example: You have 3.65 lots of GBP and 5.26 lots of CHF at 12.5%. 7.5% gives you 2.19 GBP and 3.15 CHF. All you need to do is sell 1.46 GBP and 2.11 of CHF.

Keep in mind you probably bought currencies at different rates, so you will need to average them out to let the Manager know what you own.

c. Choose to eliminate a currency because one of them hit a major Resistance.

Example: The Euro hit an all time high and you know the retracement is imminent.

The Allocator will tell you the exact lots needed to hedge the Pound against the Franc. Sell your Euros, and then buy more Pounds and more Francs. You may want to average the prices out first, as the "approximate" prices will be way off.

2. Your Equity Just Lost a Lot of Money

Let's say you are suddenly down 64% on your Equity. Once again, this is not the Holy Grail, it is the Forex market. It is a $2 trillion/day market and it's as wild as it gets. Anything can happen. That's why we have all those caution warnings. Acknowledge them as they are important.

There will always be Fundamental reasons for this: gas prices increase, a war begins, there is a business scare in China, the value of gold drops drastically. Basically, the mirror of FreedomRocks is broken. You knew it was not 100%. Remember, a 97% mirror on a yearly basis sometimes becomes 84% monthly, which is why you want a low Margin Percentage.

a. Add money

Adding money is not my favorite choice. This is when you add money on a heavy downtrend. The bottom line is simple; the market is going down heavily and you almost lost your Equity. Would you invest in this market at this particular time?
I wouldn't. It's better to wait to see some proof of a reversal, not just a retracement.

My good friend, Ken, is a Trader. He backtested this theory. He said that if he had started with $25k on September 10, 2001 (a day before 9/11) using FreedomRocks, with the Pound against the Franc at 12%, he would have ended with -$81k on September 13th.

In my opinion, a Margin Call can be your friend with proper Money Management. If it does come up, it's time to sit back and wait for it to pass, unless you want to hedge that position. Adding good money behind bad money is like "bucking the trend." It can be suicidal. Let this trend pass. The market will come back to normal again and you may make the money you lost in no time at all.

b. Close it all

Just for a second, imagine what would happen if a natural disaster or a war were to strike -- the market might drop faster than you could get out. Remember, there is a possibility of you owing more money than invested.

If the market gaps down during a weekend, the broker's platform has no way to Margin Call you, since the market is closed. You may end up on Sunday afternoon with an ugly debt to the broker.

It's one of the reasons I rarely open a position on Fridays. Sometimes I don't even open on Thursdays, unless it is a quick day trade. I don't think it's worth the risk.

Don't be afraid of taking losses. It's better to lose $1,000 now than $5,000 in thirty minutes from now. Sometimes, Traders go into paralysis as they start praying for the market to come back. Get out. You will catch it back on the next reversal and recoup the money you lost. It's only a matter of time. Capital preservation is always, always your first objective.

c. Reduce Margin Percentage
If it seems to be a "normal" day of activity in market behavior, and if you have time, you can reduce your Margin Percentage by reducing your positions evenly between the currencies. Check how much a new reduced allocation will give you, then take off some positions accordingly.

d. Merge with another currency
The Yen and the Pound are more volatile than the Franc and the Euro. If you are just trading one (or worse, two) volatile currencies, you may want to

merge a more stable one so you slow down the volatility.

Before you make any of these decisions, it's important to check the Technicals and see what the story is there. If you see a Doji on a daily chart, or if you just bottomed on a 50% Fibo, you may just want to hang in there. When my EUR/CHF was down 64% (May 14, 2006), I knew there were no major mirrors broken and it was just a matter of time for the Equity to come back. Sure enough, a few weeks later my account was 24% positive. Similarly, after five weeks, on September 21, 2006 (the evening of the first FreedomRocks convention), my Equity exploded to 40%.

The daily chart showed a major Doji. A long-term Resistance was pips away and my Intuition indicator was clear it would fall.

The next day, my profit went from 40% to 16%. This is one of the reasons I researched ways of fine-tuning the system. I created Money Management strategies and thus began writing this manual.

Pipville wasn't built in a day.

Burt Mulwitz
Notable Investor

IX. Margin Call

Some people have asked, "Is the FreedomRocks system perfect?" *Of course not!* Mark Vincellette is the first to say so. Depending on the Margin Percentage selected, you will have more or less Margin Calls. Eventually, one will hit you in the face and it can hurt if you are just starting with your original investment.

You see, the goal is to stay alive, period! As I said previously, it's all about capital preservation. The winnings will take care of itself, big time. So, what could break the hedge that is created when we buy currencies that mirror each other?

First of all, we know the mirror is not 100% and that it varies month to month and year to year. You can expect, in a historically 98% (Euro) mirror situation, a 2% non-correlation. This is when you will see periods where it will be all good or all bad. Your Equity is going to head for the sky or drop to the Margin Call. If the mirror were perfect, the EUR/CHF would be a straight, flat line.

As I have stated before, out of the four currencies offered by FreedomRocks, I only deal with the three Amigos, (EUR, GBP and CHF).

The YEN, while offering a very tempting Carry Trade opportunity, has no ties with Europe and, as such, has a correlation limited only to the common peg, the US dollar.

At the time of this writing, the Carry Trade is very positive between the USD/CHF, even if you use the Three Amigos. You can get approximately 45% per year just on the Carry Trade, provided of course, you use a 400:1 leverage and a 10% Margin Percentage maximum. The exception would be if you have doubled your money and want to be more aggressive. Remember, the Margin Percentage is the portion of your Equity that is actually buying currencies. The rest (90% in this case) will act as a buffer when the correlation is not perfect.

Fig. 23 shows the chart in February 2007 with the warning signs of a reversal. On this Daily Chart, Parabolics reversed with many other warning signs. I hedged my GBP/USD & EUR/USD buys, selling the same amount of lots in GBP/CHF.

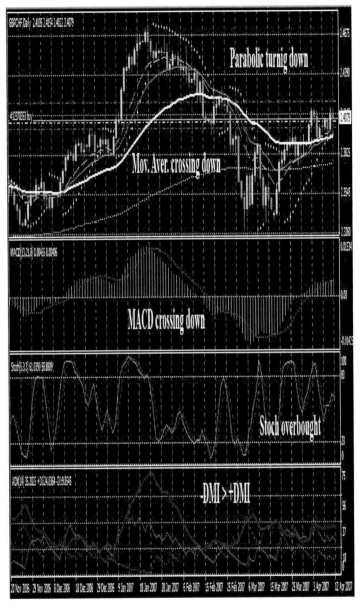

Fig. 23

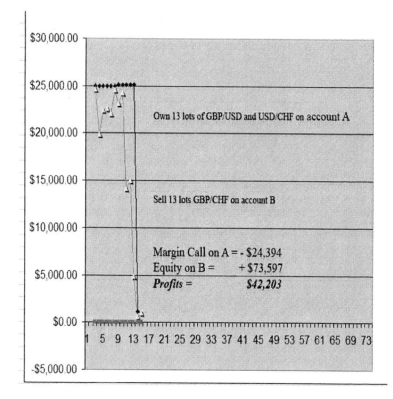

Fig. 24

Fig. 24 shows a test on a Demo account through the steep downtrend at the end of February 2007. While a $25k account got a Margin Call at 16.88%, the short side made $73,597 generating an overall profit of over $40,000.

In the graph above, I used the same lots on the short side (B) that I had from the Allocator (A). As you can see, it came out far too profitable. The idea, when profiting from a Margin Call, is not to turn it

72

around and make a fortune, but to come out even or slightly better. Remember, hedging that way has the risk of turning the account back to normal. Account B will cost more than account A is trying to recoup. In this situation, it looks like one can sell half the lots owned to break even.

This example shows why trading at above 13% Margin Percentage is very risky. It is advisable to stay under 12.5%, and preferably under 10%. In fact, when I trade amounts above $50,000, I get even more conservative and stay at around 5%.

Beware of greed; the market has very little forgiveness for misplaced emotions.

Reggie Henkart
Forex Trainer

X. Money Management

> *Every winner needs to master three essential components of trading: a sound individual psychology, a logical system and a good money management plan. These essentials are like three legs of a stool – remove one and the stool will fall, together with the person who sits on it.*
>
> Dr. Alexander Elder
> Author of *Trading For A Living*

In the quote above, Dr. Elder talks about three components of trading. Mastering these elements will guarantee your success. They are Psychology, System and Money Management. Let's go through them one-by-one.

1. Psychology

To some extent, FreedomRocks covers most of the psychology component for you. When you don't have to think or evaluate what has to be done and when you stick to the plan (because you have no choice), psychology will have very little control over you. If, however, you want to trade FreedomRocks by choosing entries and exits, changing currencies or Margin Percentages, you will have to control your emotions.

Greed, fear, revenge or being cocky can get you into trouble. Now remember, it's typically greed or fear that decided what level of Margin Percentage you started at in the first place. The tug of war between these two elements will determine your level of participation.

Why are people so much more successful trading any market on a Demo account than a Live account?

Mark Douglas in *Trading in the Zone,* says: *"When it comes to trading, your fears will act against you in such a way that you will cause the very thing you are afraid of to actually happen. If you're afraid of being wrong, your fear will act upon your perception of market information in a way that will cause you to do something that ends up making you wrong."* In a Demo account, there is no fear. It's like playing Poker with matches, no money is involved.

When my account was negative 64%, fear could have caused me to close my positions so I wouldn't lose more. My belief in the program made me stay in the market, and I was over 24% just a few weeks later.

2. System

The second component of trading is having a great system. FreedomRocks takes care of that as well.

The system is already in place. Buying two or three currencies that mirror each other, will give you the hedge (no stop loss needed). Profits are three fold: leveraged interest rates, positive trades and high Equity swings (Fig. 25).

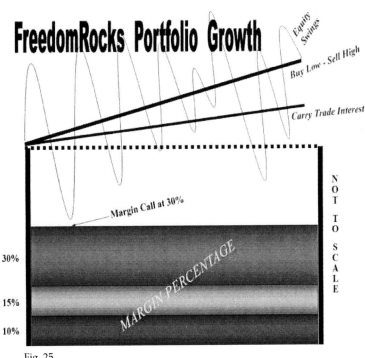

Fig. 25

There are three ways of making money in FreedomRocks:
- **Carry Trade** given by the Allocator in interest form
- **Buy Low – Sell High** given by the Manager in Pending Order form

- **Equity Swings** given by the Market when the mirror is not perfect. It can work for you as I demonstrated in a previous example of 50% in 4 weeks. Or it can work against you with a downtrend and possibly, a Margin Call.

3. Money Management

The last component is Money Management, which will allow you to be one of the few successful Traders in this wild, two trillion dollar per day market.

The secret is to cash out. Your first goal is to get to the level where it is not your money that is in the market.

Once you double your original investment, you ask the broker to pay you back that investment. The portion left in the market, your profit, is Other People's Money (OPM).

How concerned will you be when you are not investing your own hard-earned money? Fear may have very little grip on your decisions, but greed still might. Watch out for greed, as you don't want to start being reckless on the sole pretext that it's not your money.

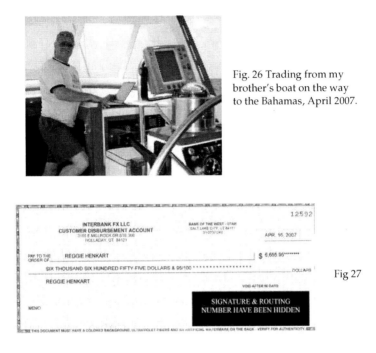

Fig. 26 Trading from my brother's boat on the way to the Bahamas, April 2007.

Fig 27

After 18 days, I made 26% and asked IBFX to send me my profit of $6655.95 (see Fig. 27). Not bad for a two week sailing trip! This check is an example of when to take profit. You want to *"cut your losses short and let your profits run."* In this case, I asked the broker to send me a check as I made over 25%. You do that four times, and the money left in the account is Other People's Money (OPM). It's a very comfortable place to be trading from.

In my opinion, it does not make sense to "cash grab" at around 5%. You will pay more fees to the broker and re-allocate all the time.

Fig. 28 Typical 4 weeks in FreedomRocks if you select entries and exits.

PAST PERFORMANCES DO NOT GUARANTEE
FUTURE RESULTS - www.ezfx.biz

DATE	BALANCE	BAL. %	EQUITY	EQU. %
11/29/06	$100,000.00	0.00%	$99,865	-0.14%
12/1/06	$101,120.19	1.12%	$109,123	9.12%
12/7/06	$101,120.19	1.12%	$96,216	-3.78%
12/8/06	$101,120.19	1.12%	$102,827	2.83%
12/11/06	$102,116.46	2.12%	$99,923	-0.08%
12/12/06	$112,213.61	12.21%	$112,214	12.21%
12/13/06	$112,213.61	12.21%	$111,456	11.46%
12/13/06	$112,213.61	12.21%	$111,456	11.46%
12/14/06	$112,213.61	12.21%	$118,094	18.09%
12/14/06	$118,059.89	18.06%	$118,060	18.06%
1/3/07	$118,059.89	18.06%	$116,874	16.87%
1/4/07	$118,059.89	18.06%	$112,689	12.69%
1/5/07	$119,306.27	19.31%	$105,981	5.98%
1/11/07	$121,075.99	21.08%	$129,850	29.85%
1/12/07	$121,075.99	21.08%	$138,648	38.65%
1/15/07	$121,186.66	21.19%	$141,504	41.50%

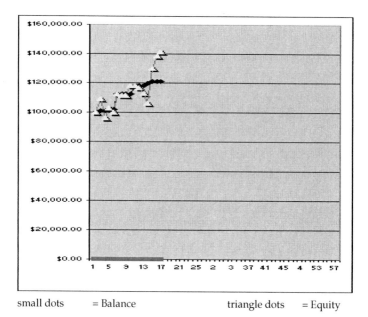

small dots = Balance   triangle dots = Equity

A dear friend of mine borrowed $5,000 from his credit card (a no-no in any kind of investing) and a few FreedomRocks months later had $30,000. He was very lucky, as he could have lost his $5,000 in a few days. I told him to take some cash out, pay back his credit card and leave only OPM. I hope he did as a few weeks later, we had the China scare in February 2007.

The China scare was the first major drawdown since FreedomRocks started its system in the Forex market in November 2005. Some Traders had a problem cutting their losses and had a Margin Call.

There is a rumor in FreedomRocks that says you need to leave your losses in so they can recoup later. Let me ask you this, what is the difference between cashing out with a loss and reinvesting in the same way, or leaving your money where it is? The only one I see is that you will pay the spread to the broker. So here is a thought: if you see you are in a position when *you would not invest at that moment,* get out! That is where the "Cut your losses short" comes in. You can always invest again later when the market is more favorable. You won't win a prize by adding to your losses. Step back and see the entire forest, not just the trees.

When I am not using FreedomRocks, my stop losses are about 2% of my Equity. With FreedomRocks, there are no stop losses.

I design my Margin Percentages in four phases. The idea is to quickly double my money so the money at risk will only be from my profits.

I based this on my favorite selection, the Three Amigos: Pound, Euro and Franc at 400:1. This example starts with $10,000 of your money. Re-allocating steps are 50-100% of your Equity.

Since the Euro was introduced in 1998, most Margin Calls were hitting down to 13.5%. This is why you don't want to go over a 12.5% Margin Percentage (and you would only go there if you use OPM).

Some drastic downtrends, as the one created by the tragedy of 9/11, will destroy your account no matter what your percentage is at.

Remember:
OPM = Other People's Money
R-A = Re-Allocate

Invest	**Margin**	**R-A**	**Cash Out**
1. Pre-OPM, on an R-A of 50%			
10k	7.5-10%	15k	5k
10k	7.5-10%	15k	5k
2. OPM, on an R-A of 100%			
10k	10-12.5%	20k	5k
15k	10-12.5%	30k	5k
25k	10-12.5%	50k	5k
45k	10-12.5%	90k	10k
3. Post-OPM, on an R-A of 50%			
80k	5-7.5%	120k	20k
100k	5-7.5%	150k	50k

4. Repeat last line with 100k until you get a Margin Call

What determines a percentage between a minimum and a maximum is the amount of interest you want to receive. In other words, you can select your interest in the Portfolio Allocator. You want to limit yourself between the suggested brackets. Keep in mind that, as your Balance grows, your Margin Percentage will diminish, hence reducing your risks.

Conclusion

FreedomRocks is an amazing program that was set up very well. It has proven itself through thousands and thousands of trades. At this time, there are over 5,000 members in over 80 countries, some investing over a million dollars in this strategy.

The good news is that you don't have to re-invent the wheel or use any of the techniques or indicators explained in this book. It all works very well just as it is. Just make sure you are very careful with your Margin Percentage and your Money Management.

Mark Vincellette always enters the market on a Wednesday, taking advantage of Triple Interest Day, regardless of Technicals or Fundamentals. He made 233% in 2006 without any other tools than FreedomRocks.

My friend, Franklin Johnson, once asked his students, *"Are you looking to trade or looking for a trade?"* In other words, don't go into the market because you have an urge to trade. Jump in only when it is the perfect time for the system you are using.

I hope this book has been helpful and educational. If you have more questions, you can always reach me at <u>reggie@4XEZ.biz</u>.

Think smart and have many productive pipping days.

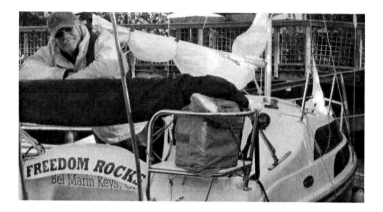

Fig. 29 "Fair winds to all of you. Freedom definitely *Rocks!*"

Reggie Henkart
Bel Marin Keys, CA
June 2007

Bibliography

So many great books have been written on trading. I could fill pages and pages with a list that probably would overwhelm you. Instead, I selected five of my favorites, not in any particular order. I highly recommend that you read them all.

- *Technical Analysis of the Financial Markets,* by John Murphy (NYIF 1999).
- *The Candlestick Course,* by Steve Nison (A Marketplace Book 2003).
- *Day Trading the Currency Market,* by Kathy Lien (Wiley 2006).
- *Trading in the Zone,* by Mark Douglas (NYIF 2000).
- *Trading for a Living,* by Dr. Alexander Elder (Wiley 1993).

The magazines I read include:
- *Technical Analysis of Stocks & Commodities.*
- *The Economist.*

About the Author

 Reggie Henkart was born in Belgium to a family that included an *"agent de change,"* (Foreign Exchange Trader).

In the early 90's, he was hired as a Forex Fund Manager by Frankwell Investment Services in San Francisco. Reggie was responsible for several quarter million dollar accounts and was quickly promoted from Trader to Trainer, supervising 20 Traders on his team. The company sent him to Hong Kong and Canton where he was recognized as a top leader.

In February 2006, he was introduced to a company called FreedomRocks and quickly became one of the top ten earners in the company, building his business in over 10 countries. Within one year, he held approximately 25% of the company's membership.

Reggie teaches at the Learning Annex in San Francisco and conducts his own highly acclaimed classes. His newsletter, *The Spot Review*, reaches Traders around the globe. He occasionally hosts webinars at www.FxStreet.com.

Reggie resides in Marin County, CA with his wife Andrea. He's the proud father of two grown children, Journey and Quest.